"Translation, transformation, echo, recall, recollection, migration — Ariel Resnikoff makes diaspora home in these multilexical, iconoclastic, antic lyrics, blessings, and curses. 'Held in the ancient footlights of time.'"

—Charles Bernstein, author of *Near/Miss*

"If transliterated from Hebrew and Aramaic 'od' is a 'going around…with force and abundance,' with ferocity and sensorial luxuriance, Ariel Resnikoff's *Unnatural Bird Migrator* erupts as not just 'odd practices of a false messiah', but a force-filled prescient lament and celebration of translingual possession, procession, precession; marked by licks' spit, split-tongued myths, rituals prayers, rasps, gasps, rattles ciphers seeds, spells where every letter is a universe, hovering through incantatory chants of radical hybridity."

—Adeena Karasick, author of *Salomé: Woman of Valor*

"*Unnatural Bird Migrator* is a book that's got kishkes [lit. guts]. Ariel Resnikoff creates a midrashic translingual poetics that joins ancestral echoes with contemporary lyric, where inherited speech is never without questioning or transgression. Through 'poetic deformance,' the reader is pushed to 'notice/who speaks & who is spoken,' as the biblical collides with the new. *Unnatural Bird Migrator* excavates the gaps between languages (Yiddish-, Hebrew-, Aramaic-, Akkadian- Englishes) so that 'we are disoriented, finally,' able to see poem as 'perpetual displacement' incantatory in all the best ways."

—erica kaufman, author of *Post Classic*

"Wreaking havoc on the unity of an ur-language and the Book of books, that formidable repository of truth and authenticity, *Unnatural Bird Migrator* runs the gamut from a Schwerner-esque rendering of lower-case tablets (Resnikoff's translinguistic transcreations from Aramaic and Hebrew to Akkadian and Yiddish) to paratactic surveys of Middle East politics (where 'the land is not invented tho the claim to/ owning it is') and contemporary Jewish life. Installing as many differences as he raises, Resnikoff insists that since 'the border is a grammar built on power,' the agrammatical allows us to see that 'this is just on the other side of this.' Crossing back and forth between the real and the false, faith and heresy, *Unnatural Bird Migrator* refuses all modes of piety, reminding us 'how a single prayer springs to language, resting btwn tongue &/ tooth momentarily, sways a military buoy…'A leveled Babel all too pertinent for our time, *Unnatural Bird Migrator* explodes the semantic field of every language it engorges."

—**Tyrone Williams, author of *As iZ***

the operating system
glossarium / unsilenced texts
print//document

UNNATURAL BIRD MIGRATOR

ISBN 978-1-946031-87-7
Library of Congress Control Number 2020935471

copyright © 2020 by Ariel Resnikoff
designed by Riv Weinstock with the OS Open Design Protocol
edited by ELÆ [Lynne DeSilva-Johnson] and Riv Weinstock

As of 2020 all titles are available for donation-only download via our Open Access Library: www.theoperatingsystem.org/os-open-access-community-publications-library/

This text was set in Freight Sans, beer money, Minion and Narkisim.
Cover art: Michael Sgan-Cohen
קן לציפור, כן לציפור, דרור לציפור
Unnatural Bird Migrator
Silkscreen & Acrylic on paper, 1983
(c) Courtesy of the Artist's Estate

the operating system
brooklyn & worldwide
www.theoperatingsystem.org

UNNATURAL BIRD MIGRATOR

Ariel Resnikoff

nest of the bird

yes to the bird

liberation of the bird

For Rivkale, Feygele &
Zamir Shulem Ernest
&
In memory of Michael Sgan-Cohen

א

YINGLOSSIA

ב

FROMSHIBBOLETH

CONTENTS

LICK & SPIT:
TRANSINCANTATIONS

ג

DAYBOOKS

AVOIDANCES

ד

CODA: EVERY NEW POET

An old old saying I invented tomorrow as a spanking new proverb & that will be true yesterday too has it in something close to English — wherever that may be — that "exile is the only home we have" & says something different in all the other languages I can & cannot translate it into & from, or as this book puts it: "abstracted exiles alphabetic." It is, I think, one way, and maybe a useful way, into Ariel Resnikoff's *Unnatural Bird Migrator.*

What the book makes clear is what we should have known all along: there is no original language, Babel Babble is the multiple lingo-stew in the skull-pot of that mensch clambers up onto the stage known as the anthroposcene. Scary? Yes. As an aside, and beyond the sheer pleasure I have always taken in the confusarium of our smelting pot of lingos — one reason obviously why I delight so much in the book at hand — I myself have always wo-ndered/wo-rried: wo, wo, what if my last sentence would be in my first language which no one around me speaks anymore & with me leaving the scene, who'd be there to translate? That thought came back about half-way through the book, at the end of the Yinglossiads (should be "Yinglossias" as the plural of "Yinglossia" but "…iads" came naturally as defining a new poetic genre, possibly). A thought followed shortly after by the suggestion that maybe I could point to the word "Exile" on my forearm, my only tattoo — if you can read Arabic, neither my first nor my last language. And as I read on, I recalled the strange joy I experienced on a flight from New York to somewhere that was not yet the afterlife when the little screen in front of me gave this response to a now forgotten query: "Please wait. The language you have requested is being processed."

Even if this book often throws me back to my own stammers & lingo-stews, it first of all & mainly exhilarates by its necessary daring in that it is a cutting-edge act of "investigative poetry," to use Ed Sanders' term. *Unnatural Bird Migrator* powerfully combines investigations of the innards, organs, offal & "prime cuts" of the haram, kosher, halal & terefah languages we have & use & misuse, with the ways they are engraved, tattooed, incised on the living skin of 'istorin, history as what I & you participate in by walking & being in the places that matter, that is, in/on borders everywhere. All places are, by the way, borders. If there is, as I said above, no original language, then all is translation, thus movement over ever-changing terrain, & thus all terrain becomes an in-between, a border that needs to be sensed & sentenced (not to life but to live) with & in such ever-changing lingo-mutations, the only *tekné* able to scout & report accurately from there, I mean from here, right now.

How does Ariel Resnikoff get to what I call a "nomad poetics?" Let me quote him from an interview he gave to Tinge Magazine: "My life moves through multiple languages — that's the first thing. Throughout the day, whether in books, letters, or live conversations, I toggle between English, Hebrew, Yiddish & Spanish. Sometimes I go to French, sometimes to German. Sometimes I find myself in Aramaic. I am not interested at any level of my language practice in what monolingual ideological interests call 'fluency'; & perhaps this is one of the reasons I became a poet, to avoid the violence that fluency inflicts on my everyday language practice. In poetry, I discovered a whole slew of writers who, like me, have found themselves in exile from/in multiple languages at once & who use poetry as a tool of survival. How absurd, says the 'self-exiled' high modernist — but it's true; when you have no language at all to call your own, the role of poetry becomes first & foremost a question of need."

We could now go & quote the likes of Derrida (*je n'ai qu'une langue, or ce n'est pas la mienne*, a formula he shares with Celan, but that I, & I think Ariel Resnikoff too, would dispute) or closer to home, agree with Charles Bernstein (that poetry, with written language as its medium, is, in fact, the exploration and realization of the human common ground of 'us', in which we are), but let me just briefly insist on this: given that we know that all languages are foreign languages, we need to keep in mind what Lawrence Venuti said: "The worst thing you can do with foreign writing is to treat it like a pet — by domesticating it." Resnikoff's writing is proof of this, & teaches us to let the languages run wild, to play & joke & dance with them, & thus let them teach us their moves.

Then the poet writes (exclaims? jubilates? worries? stammers?) that "to escape the perpetual torments inflicted upon it the dybbuk-tongue seeks refuge in a garbled mouth…" but happy, I believe, that "we are disoriented, finally" — which is most useful as long as it doesn't mean we are (to be) re-occidented: there are many more directions we can & have to travel in, just look & you can lick the darkness eyes open wide border (on) the real, spike it with garlic-words, now go read these poems. Because as Ariel Resnikoff has it "for someone like me, or any of us who physically feel the breaking terrain of language beneath our feet, poetry is a temporary & necessary dwelling in the most ceremonial sense." I hope "temporary" here means a very long time: "May [h]e fan forever the shekhina embers"!

Pierre Joris
Victor, Montana
October 13, 2020

& here I recall in the migration of the storks in
their eastward season, & we the children used
to shout at them: "Bocianie, bocianie, pali sie
gniazdo!" — *"the stork, the stork, the nest goes up*
in flames!"

—Avot Yeshurun

God,
the cage has turned into a bird
& it has flown

—Alejandra Pizarnik

LICK&SPIT//MEMBRANECHANT

    membrane tied-up   my membrane is bent
nerve
the enchanter god sent me
    in front of šamaš i have drawn yr picture
i have traced yr figure   having observed yr
strength
        i have crafted yr appearance
        espied the shape of yr membrane i have re-
produced yr   features have bound   yr membrane & bent yr
nerves
i have done to you   the spell you did to me
    having let you under the evil-eye
        against *lek un shpy* i have let you
suffer
    my revenge   my sorcery   tricks
evil
    maleficent
    plottings   evil messages   hate's
injustice's
  murder   my paralysis of mouth
  may yr   head stop!   with the water of my membrane
& the cleansing   water of my hands   may it be spoken

& I shd know as little about it as I do   *this substance*
. . . aheym . . .
the people of substance   *for a change*   *turn the radio*
station

to the "old days [lit. years of sobyetski]   *when money*
swirled the drain

& nobody complained   *in the middle of night [lit. at the*
hour of study]

a sour odor filled the cafeteria; a stink [lit. rot]

               bad breath [lit. putrid tongue]

he is talking nonsense

is he bewildered?

[lit. taboo]
he eats as if recuperating from sickness

he is making a mess

he eats like

a horse
he is thick-headed in fog

he is squirming in horseradish
perhaps he has a cold? [lit. malaria (ague) is all

he gets]
he has nothing

he has nothing at all [lit. an itch or boil]

only, strange practices

odd ways

no say [lit. power]
a man who criticizes non-existence [lit. climbs up

walls]
he creeps like a bed-bug

doesn't know where to look

he is blind [lit. rhetorical]

ruins the language

the violent stutterer

talks into the world

he talks into sickness

talks into restlessness [lit. pins or

needles]

he is only good for fowl sacrifice [lit. worthless]
he shd go to hell

he shd meet w/ korach's death [lit. the earth
swallow him]

he is a shame to our
children
he is nothing at all

**out of which the following plan occurred [lit. standing on
one leg]

it never happened!
he never was [lit. speaking in tongues]
there still is

as in: it is not worth a knock of earth
as in: it is very cheap [lit. impossibly
expensive] the
nonsense speech [lit. deformed tongue]

cd be

it doesn't

matter
it is not becoming [lit. doesn't fit]

it fits like a slap in the face
it is the voice of a false-

messiah [lit. sarcasm] it hurts me
he appears to me

he is fainting [lit. emptied]
nothing will help

it will help like blood-cupping on a corpse

                                        it will do

it will have to
              will it heal in time for the wedding?
                                        it must

 no matter
              let us eat & be healthy

YINGLOSSIA//FIRSTSPEECH

praise god! thanks & pray. recite the 18 benedictions. *vo den*
(cut-off [lit: what else])? no sweat. god [lit. the name] respects
the humble somebody -- does he? berates the evil-ones (may
they choke on their tongues [lit. languages]). the real article is
a bargain for hire. the chew-among-chews. for rent or
(re)lease. it pleases me, see? my heart told me so, see?
i predicted it. likewise: keep it moving! don't bother me
[lit. don't throw a hook around my nose]! **a stutterer was
seen as a scatterbrain, confuser, & somehow also a conniver,
twister, self-promoter, not to be trusted [lit. jew]. human dung
was attributed to [lit. the inferior merchandise]. now we talk
excessively or not at all. a groan, maybe, even, a disparaging
sigh…cd be…lies on the square & still talking non-sense

YINGLOSSIA//FRIENDLYFACE

friendly face. a familiar face.
like a hot bath. like a bowl of chopped meat.
stop banging on my head [lit. bargaining w/ my sanity]
the gargling solution shd be
fresh breath? o, that it shd come true!
who bringeth forth bread from the earth, etc.
to the common people, for a bargain say, not only to do
business but for heartache, see? sweetheart (singing) *my heart's*
love is a pit in the earth . . .
listen: you can shake-stammer
in impending fire
from stuffed cabbage to stuffed cabbage to
stuffed (*holebshes/holishkes/holubtshe*) depending on
from-where.
& so I made a mistake. so the words abrade. so what?
i've been called worse than debauchee
many times before, a caine-raiser
carouser, mad man, mongrel, kyke --

YINGLOSSIA//
DOWNTHEOLDHATCH

for LZ

i.
down the old hatch, skol! -- & up my white mouth, onto bib,
fringed scrap covered mist [lit. refuse]; I was spewing litvish
"funereal" shrewdness against the wall: a black [lit. singed]
magic transcription [lit. false-messiah]

ii.
which one arrives at when one has no business left to tend --
no trade, calling, nor income -- when one is forced to live by
improvisation alone, drawing livelihood "from the air" --
& not achieving anything, but starving by our wits

iii.
come to the point
[lit. make it sharp!]

scream like hell
[lit. spill yr guts]

curse the name
[lit. ruin yrself]

                --what's the difference? [lit. as is typically recited by
the youngest child]

\\\ 32 \\\ |

YINGLOSSIA//LIZARDSLAUGH

**the expert-connoisseur know-it-all brings a boil from the cut
inf(l)ected tongue to the inspector-overseer of kashrus:

it's my own fault, I know [lit. I cooked it]. might vomit from
the smell of it, but can't get rid of it . . .

it's delicious [lit. the lizards laugh] -- they don't let you live!

talk & talk & talk yr tongue off! it is said that a jew who works
on the sabbath [lit. an invalid] is not fit to suck a ham. the long
meaningless rigmarole [slang, lit. scroll of esther] implanted in
my speech --

o forget it! you're nothing more than a derelict nibbler
[lit. sweet tooth]:

sweetheart darling child in me -- sweet little soul in me -- what
difference does it make whether we live or die? the inf(l)ected
tongue -- may it keep its distance! & the impure food [slang,
lit. pig feed] doesn't do a thing. not today & not tomorrow
[lit. never after the closing prayer], but out of thin air hangs on.
now only god knows . . . so? well? move it along already!
hurry up! aren't you done yet?

YINGLOSSIA//MINKHE

for Anne Tardos

in praise & submission to a baby-son [yiddishism (derisive)] --
let us prepare the tools for extraction [lit. from tongues]. if the
fever is of a jewish head -- is it a shaygets luck? There's no evil
eye, either way, as they say (*tu-tu*), the canary keep away. single
men of marriageable age [lit. little birds] crumpled into misfits
for a spoiled lap of milk, narrowly achieved [lit. hardly lived to
see] the transformation of soars into sacrifice (slang [lit. false-
messianism]). raw groats (a mess-up [lit. mix-up of]) & cooked
groats w/ broad noodles at a kosher boarding-house-cafeteria in
the far-reaches of the Bronx [lit. a lively Russian dance, usually
to sexual cause (ie. of 'blind mixing')]. in amulet [lit. charm,
(from german, "*kind-bet-tzettel*")] worn at birth, containing
psalm 121: *di nomen fun melokhim* [lit. names of angels] -- a
vision of god, in-labor, & after, old & young, eating plates of
stuffed derma (in flour & onion, salt, feffer & shmaltz, (to keep
them in skins) -- the ticklish little prigs (technically, talkative
little jews [lit. fruitless idle questions)]: not in "reality," so to say
[lit. "as if it were" (pronounced *ver*)], round dumplings made of
groat-meal cooked-up in pork belly stew & tied at the corners
in 'bakers handkerchiefs.' dumplings filled w/ potatoes & livers,
kidneys & barley: a petulant excitability by a gad-about gang of
jews gathers about --"he had been perfect [lit. legitimate] before
the cross-eyed sickness took!" first in small pockets of dough
filled w/ meat & curd-cheese, the magic-worker, trickster,
phony casper milquetoast corrupts the root-canals of the pure
jewish jaw. a virus of the tongue & teeth [lit. cheek & mouth].
                    how does it inf(l)ect?

**in force of false laughter & aguish [lit. idling], the loafer lox-addict stutterer stumbles out of the afternoon prayer-hall, wreathing in false thanks & praise: "may we fan forever the *shekhina* embers"! [lit. blessed is the vessel as it breaks]

YINGLOSSIA//BLESSEDAREWE

go away! go hump w/ the whales (peddle yr fish elsewhere
[lit. whistle at a leviathan]).
go to hell! [lit. may you choke on yr tongue] shit in the ocean.
spill yr guts.
spill yr guts against the city hall.
spill yr guts against the synagogue [lit. house-of-entry]
that you shd threaten the "holy geese" upon entering (& don't
frighten me [lit. you little non-native jew of galicia])!
someone hollers: go frig yrself . . .
the same to you! [hebraism, lit. big deal… (derisive)]
quite well, huh? tho it doesn't work-out the way we planned.
there is no "complete man" to bribe, see?
blessed are we, w/ children & all (in fractured
English [lit. utter misery])
we are chopped-in w/ the herring & vodka [lit. minced]

YINGLOSSIA//FIRSTBURIAL

i'm dying for it [lit. my soul expiring] -- that delicacy called
'bad taste.' as an old bumbling hebrew teacher is w/out
his *heder* [lit. one room school] -- i am called unpalatable
[lit. soured] & accused of crazy fowl chatter-cracklings.
called crazy kyke & sold from house to house [lit. kosherly
butchered] at a bargain

for as the light said unto me, unto you there shall be a tiny box
henceforth containing 2 tiny portions of deuteronomy (vi. 4-9
& xi. 13-2) lines handwritten on a goatskin parchment in 22
tongues

it doesn't frighten me, see? i'm not having it, see?
& perhaps on account of the indoor bath they call *mikve*
[lit. purity] or what?
a dietary constraint that cuts between food?
or what? yr cutlery kept separate?
or what?
only *milkhig* utensils?
or what?
a quorum of men holding worship?
or what?

try harder! recite the 18 prayers!
or what?
one way or (an)other.
w/out promise [lit untruthfully] speaking in

YINGLOSSIA//MOYLSONG

the designator of disbelief in distaste & contempt for the navel
pupick penis urinator [lit. piss] male infant—for an
un-fortunate no-one [lit. little squirt] pee-pot
(slang, [lit. ugly or interrupting])—in fumbled lock-jaw catch.
a gutteral sputtering snort: "boor, mutter, mumbler

YINGLOSSIA//REBITSN\\REBBE

he who "compassions mercy": rabbi, mister rabbi, *dear* . . !
(it was the rabbi's wife
's almost sarcastically over-pious [lit. to shout & get no answer]
whispering
thru the slats: "for all the good it'll do ya --

the inflammatory sickness starts
in the mouth & works its way up. doesn't bother w/ IOUs. pays
cash in advance.

o, god in heaven, master of the universe—who knows if he's the
real mccoy…! this "nervous" body talking non-sense, cd just as
soon be acting out a part

as he who "goes to the devil" [lit. speaks in tongues]—a tooth
into his mother's toe . . . (forgive me (or do I mis-speak? they
call me violent names "in a language of rags"; "the wandering
kyke"—*bite yr tongue!*

YINGLOSSIA//COMMONSENSE

for Ted Greenwald

what a..! what kind of a..! what's it matter to you, *huh*? now
don't get excited [lit. burst into flame]. it stinks—what're
you talking? smack smack (gently said) wd you keep quiet?
(shouted), quiet, I said, shutup! there's the professional
(professorial) type who makes a living from it, gathering the
pious sheep, berating the irreligious who "flout" the sacred law.
"beautiful as the seven worlds," (belles lettres, & w/ a hearty
laugh [lit. half-sarcastically]). the wig at the wedding she wore
ever after (a watchword greeting, beadle at the *shtibl* quoting
old policeman's slang: "it had been a brothel whorehouse
(before) mix of wool & linen!" now you oughta be ashamed
of yrself [lit. to the bottom of yr throat]. the prettier ones they
bury [lit. this one is an ugly one]. & gather pleasure, the little
nothings for a "messenger drunkard" non-jewish [lit. impious
or wild one]. if to skin one: a hag-mare worthless one [lit.
mischievous child] or apoplectic wreck. where the customer
is king [americanism], a snake can also be a shrew clumsy
bungler, drag, poor luckless sponger, butter-fingered shmock

YINGLOSSIA//PARVENU

so now, get rid of it:
alas for a lack, woe unto *whom*?
either too much or too little [lit. a wallop or a toot]
"dear me!" (imitatingly —*parvenu*!
cut it short [lit. w/out intro(duction)]
conceited & peevish
sulky & stuffed in a puffy shirt
tired-out
& sputtered as confused
little pups [lit. overly made-up]
"the rich are too stuffed-up
to photograph [lit. stuffed in dead birds]
& drunk
me bothersome hanger-on
cursing in
disorderly
survival

YINGLOSSIA//
BEHINDTHESCHOLA

for Pierre Joris

**quick quickly, the beggar watchman elijah cuts young mens'
pious at an all-time-low: "now cut it short!"
have you finished the dirty work?
pins & needles in his toe (a spanking-new proverb preaching
another wretched thing:

       just think how it reflects
on the religious
democrazy! the very rich [lit. stone rich] strong & brave,
shitting sorrel grass
soup—piece-pits in a leafy green stew (yiddishism,

      idiomatic for those inclined to heretics: "one who

      becomes dumb like a piece of wood" [lit. loses speech])
—tell the children's children! some fool. a bit of piece tricks the
smaller bits toward quiet death. prideful sweet-cakes in skin-
thin dough rolled-up
in blue cheese & rotted beef: w/ push-shove vulgarism: *vilde
khaye* [lit. wild beast]. behind the schola in a snored aside:
a bent new year! it's gone -- it doesn't matter. the sour cream's
always all ready & sour. finally (pronounced *phew*)! listen --
hold on -- how's this

the flavor -- a good taste, really -- is that so? *tokhes oyfn tish*
[lit. ass on the grass]. well certainly & each w/ small cakes
dipped in ham-baked-cheese carried under 7 rectangular
prayer-shawls btwn the study hall's walls. the complete deluxe
treasury of chewish law –- commandments i study at yr feet.
naïve, simple minded: a feeble big nose -- big deal!
but in a language of rags . . .

**during the ceremony of casting off of sins (crumbs of stale
bread into a stream) the father papa daddy-dear or tateniu:
my dear impossibly costly one -- y're simply unattainable [lit.
the moon on a plate]. a dullard bethrothal we put up (or shut
up) [lit. ass on the grass] day-to-day good-for-nothing dead-
starved & drunk

YINGLOSSIA//ACUTEPAIN

for Jerome Rothenberg

a cute pain, usually appearing as *oi vai zmir* [lit. woah is me]
--the stuff & nonsense air, so you say [lit. know from what].
in crawling ache [slang, lit. wandering jew] & never stopped to
itch. but whom are you kidding? [lit. what's the joke?] & whom
are you fooling? [lit. who're you fucking over (this time)?]
when I eat my anti-semites, i'll chew them out myself. they're
jews like me. i'm hell on earth to them. gaping as a pit
[lit. where the devil sits to say his mourning prayers]; *get*
killed! they recite (in communal prayer); *drop dead! get lost!*
go choke on yrself
. . . who knows? who cd've believed? to be ruined as such
[lit. inf(l)ected]. how's business? how's tricks? what's yr name,
huh? what's yr mother's name? how come? how much? (a wild
one). . .you want? what else? what's it matter (to me), huh?
what're you talking my head off? watch out! [lit. to throw one's
eye] what a sober carries on his lung, a drunk struts- but what's
the difference? capable of [lit. what's on his tongue] & all in the
cards, but what's the trick? [lit. what's cooking?] a "wound of
bologna" [lit fried sausage-cheese-noodle] or *vyzso*
[slavic, lit. fool] named for Haman's youngest son.**the jews
vooz [lit. boo] the dybuk tongue away & when sleeping, later
cut it out. photographs of the tongue are posted on the study
hall's walls to mark the day

YINGLOSSIA//SECONDBURIAL

be happy! [lit. a shapely phrase] to be at pains to make sense
amid non-sense [lit. in many tongues at once] -- excuse me? --
y're all set! [lit. back on the horse & keep riding]
blessed among an ashkenazi [lit. accent] recalling the
dead: a *mama zelig* punch, bang - pow *!* [yiddishism, thru
sexual taboo] in sparing a miserly uncouth & fake
[lit. slobbish] fate makes unruly whirring [lit. can't stop
talking] & doesn't shut its mouth. the sinner [lit. he who
tempts fate] sweet talks atop a pile of pins & bristly sticks
plotting our sins in 7-day-mourning postures [lit. a sitting
widow] patient as a shapely phrase. let it burn & may god help
[lit may god prevent] but i haven't got the faintest idea what.
so onions grow from his navel -- so what? let it be. o.k.? that's
it. let it be. if it (you) shd be so [lit. well said]. good luck & be
quiet. you shd live so [lit. in such silence]. you shd swell up like
a mountain [lit. lie in the earth].
**they place him in the ground. don't worry, *slob!*
dear son. my darling daughter

YINGLOSSIA//GOAD&NEEDLE

un-qualified & un-called for [lit. god forbid! (an old-world
deprecation to ward off evil)]—against pesty (im)possibilities
[lit. little (mis)fortunes] or tragedies bore a born-loser's luck
[lit. a jew's luck] haggart bust. butter-me-up, huh? racketeerer-
seer, huh? god forbid! *you shd goad & needle it—*

YINGLOSSIA//IMPUREBONE

good for nothing -- worth nothing -- starved [lit. dead hungry]
day-to-day contrary to the dietary laws -- forbidden foods,
impure or unprepared [lit. improvisatory] (applied also to the
sabbatean writings) in the posterior rectum [lit. buttocks-
ass, a backward variant on t*okhes*] or "house of worship". the
pashkeviln [lit. wheat-paste posters] coating the study hall's
walls: THE JEW WHO DOES NOT ABIDE BY THE JEWISH
LAW IS AN IMPURE BONE. r e a d i t & s e e (t h e) evil
inclinations [lit. those who crave pig's feed] are no-thing but
an-other ratty snot rag [yiddishism, sarcastically], decrepit
worn out no-body. said some-body to no-body, "it'd be better
to fornicate w/ one-self than to birth such a body."
said a bum ne'er-do-well faker I was -- mistaken for a petty-
paul & overdressed in wretched rags wanderings. from a
distant foreign words melted into a mouth, then confusion,
absent-minded, wild ecstatic repetition: not the one you
were expecting, but like sweet carrot pie [slang, lit. fuss over
nothing] in disgrace & humiliation hang the words on tho
unwanted, for better or worse. "do me a favor & don't do me
any favors!" the confusion agitation roister bositerer is not just
an ornamental swan, but at the fringes of language hanging-
on; & it's costly dear, too much, for such & such
[lit. bodily soars]

YINGLOSSIA//ANYHOLIDAY

spoke a coarse loud-mouth gossip: description of a man w/
indistinguishable lineage
-- a dis-connected [lit. disjointed] who threatens by
idiosyncrasy [lit. someone else's]
the other's (brand of cigarette -- *the moocher smokes . . .*
his other lung's black gaggy blabbermouth pedigree is of a
jewish head but . . . in a demon tongue? . . . managing a rusty
mourner's prayer [sung, lit. "may god remember him"]. for
festive holiday-ish sharp (referring to the tools) cd be. . . any
holy day [pronounced *yontev*, lit. a good day] or verse or re-
naming of the dead were possessed to do justice & fairness,
integrity . . . *but for a buffoon?* [lit. wild beast] strong built w/
sturdy bones & "sickly tongue," a "scampi tale" nose. beats the
alter; *we shall teach the spirits a lesson! let them leave us to our
god!* the spirits are nothing to do w/ -- but the bodies

[Note: I arrived at the present work thru a practice of translingual-poetic deformance across/between multiple code-switching dialects. My compositional method traverses by (mis) translation in/to Yiddish-, Hebrew-, Aramaic- & Akkadian-English adapted sonic/semantic properties in grammar, syntax & lexicon, taking English as its temporary "host" while performing perpetual inflectional slippages—interlingual punning & fusion-slangs—as much as the host can absorb.

The dybbuk (Yiddish: spirit-possessor), which my Jewish-Ashkenazi ancestors believed to inhabit the body of the wild stutterer, mad person, heretic or "akher" [lit. other], became the peripheral focus of this poetry. I began to imagine the "odd" transgressional practices of that other(ed) marginal antinomian ancestor —the "possessed"— & to consider the ways in which this "possession" by language might manifest in my own "odd" practices, which so mark me as poet, translator & jew. I use the word "odd" here in deliberate echo of the terms against which Sabbatean stigma was transcribed in 17th-century Palestine: "for the odd practices of a false messiah."-A.R.]

FROM SHIBBOLETH

...whose every page is an abyss
where the wing shines with the name.
—Edmond Jabès

[t h i r d   s p a c e]

for rivka, sarah, hagar

august 13, 2017 --
head to the cave of no entry
closed military zone
sign at the border
following the rd north
to a tourist zone
at the face to the head of the crag.
strange to see so many tourists on the crack
of a space which is finally
liminal. religious minion
speaking yiddish: "look up" says a father to his child "they have
telescopes to spot the arabs coming in from across the sea."
birds on a barbed wire
rock pigeon making its nest
in the grand rock cleft above us.
heat burns off into the bunker
at sunrise, mine eye is drawn to a banana orchard behind:
a man shivering in the mud.
where groups of arabs come at evening after the hundreds of
orthodox jews have departed for the night. an armenian priest
wraps in noon rock sandstone salt crossed where whitestone
angry crows nest in the cleft. days end quick despite the
tangling tourists. & what about the poisonous fish? ribs
drafting landscape via brainscape:
barbs atop the military barrack
pine needles jack in electric light.

10 men praying at the border in low ashkenazi drawl.
it is the border of poland-palestine.
a ship w/ a shooter at the helm. how a single prayer springs to
language, resting btwn tongue & tooth momentarily, sways a
military buoy

february 12, 2018 -- craw bird on border. not the same now
never the same after all. as overcast skies clouds post pulsating
grey over nakura. waves bake bleached black beaks on border
as stones foaming tide comb in too much trash to feed the
landscape. charcoal scratching fires lead water scrub on shore
rubbing stone on stone. this is just on the other side of this.
probably gone by now.
phoenician room entombed in nostalgia crabapple perch
builds cactus life behind an abandoned castle. who lived here
who can still speak? say her name — sarah.
stone on stone skeletons destroyed inhabitants. dome of bone
crows perch w/ our backs to the sea. sparks memory's sensory
seas - what do you see? pock stones below the waves break
against no signs—no passage. birds wings mark off white
launch into electric flight. sight of the site of a mass expulsion.
venetian seasons silent rains wash down interment canals. but
do not drink from them. toxic pockmarks & stone pines palm
leather cracks. no exit ahead. *no crossing at this time*

august 16, 2017 -- lebanese border fog on continuous forest. what cut by fences in leaves sway the praying persons at the border. what cut defines it? morning breeze in sound of a swimming pool filling. do you see a mosque? i see only split vines— so where are you today? time braids its dancing branches in us, splayed. just came in from. green earth & white rd leads to a lebanese bunker. i remember ted said: "split your days open four ways, sideways & timeways across the palm garden maze." facing immense marrano oceans w/ our backs to the sea. now what cut to see? birds on wing. summer red dusk dark sunrise over shtula. sabra & shatila they say for the first not murdered were raped. of necrophiliac border subsumed & death consumed in indiglo sounds of ground-shaking resin. frames sounds of jeep patrols deep underneath us. tractor capture 120 km to beirut, 250 km to jerusalem. a white flight arrives at a stark dark shuddering. the first to insist:
rosh ha-nikra — shtula — adamit

february 14, 2018 -- *arab al aramsha* -- red soil construction
plant shoot out from the inside. we wander the streets
searching for the family myzell. an old man souleiman points
us down the street: they all live at the corner of that block. tent
& view. craggy border cliff. where mother prepares dinner
while aya speaks. in 2006 a woman & her two daughters were
killed here by hezbollah katyushas. what to do with bare
facts as bare sites of violence where fight & flight both end
in unrecognizable remains? grandfather speaks as a child his
parents came on camels from Iraq. forced to confession forced
not to confess. the crimes go silent. mark the land in chalk in
dust in mud from the *shtetlekh*: here again the few have been
forced into captive. in the same breath *nakba* the same breath
khurbn, moving slowly over green pastures. hezbollah talk
on walkies— they can talk says grandfather but will never get
across. the land cut to losses cut to bureau b-role of soldiers
planting flags in the land. the land is not invented tho the
claim to owning it is. this is what grandfather teaches who
arrived on camels in tents. o brothers our sister our mothers
myzell how we love you

august 17, 2017 -- 12/G spring time at the lool smells so bad
it sounds saws & cars pass w/ men talking over clucking
hens. blue bags not here nor twd me. such a place makes me
question the ethics of eggs. afternoon heat w/ no sweat to cool
us. cement mixer mechanisms idle beside the coop. 11/A overt
questions of eggs after urn heat turns silos steel ridges silver
tipt the blue rd with no shoulder. arm with no skin. so that's
the border. narrow shoulders from muscovy finally to see a
panorama. ambulance sirens you can hear across borders you
can hear. transmission migrations solutions exclusion & fence
stone margins of rosemary at beaufort castle. i can see it from
the hill below. cameras watching at a crossing. un peacekeeping
vehicles control white vans drive to & fro between yellow flags.
from drafting landscapes in dust what it must look like to look
up. to see a face in the clouds ashen & mad. blue sky white
pages in landscape of cameras. a shooting at the border. haze i
barely see thru. bunker life underground becomes the skeleton
structure on the border chain. hazy suns on a frontier to "no-
man's" land. spin reckless border towns in silhouettes dark for
dark lights white disguise. how are the apples in the ditches?
back at home they've been burning things all day. all I can
see is the smoke. flags slapping the wind. the blast of a ram's
horn: what do you sound for in burning? soldier patrols on the
border lights grow distant dusk over lebanon. what's across the
fence? echoing

february 15, 2018 -- K/8 cawing & crawing on all sides we awake to the birds in the trees beneath us. this is the place behind the mountain. this is the place soft in ink. garden of okra & plywood. garden of graves & silverfish. garden of the names of disappeared & now invisible (*nister*). the border is a tractor in the mud. the border is a grammar built on power. the food we enjoyed grows rotten in the mouths of the border guards. sharpen yr eyes after to see where the border leads: nowhere. houses carved in caves on dead phoenician names paid in blood & snails. thin is the way the word fails. from the panhandling border of invisibility, not in purgatory but reality. morning stories grown into narrative grass & fruit small animals feed on the remains. pastures still full of remains, tho no-one remains. have gone down to the valley of screams. rasping & gasping she rattles: no escape but thru the fence

august 18, 2017 -- where water runs thru, stunned on all sides
by bird blinds they can't see. *you*, she says, as soil, the cow piles
dry-up & border flies land rubbing leg on leg. w/ vibrating
red eyes in the reeds feed the riverbanks hemorrhaging:
someone wants something to drink *but not from the stream*.
fences perch protecting trees eat red grapes from vines on
bordering plantations. the facing sun-bleached land scooches
farther as the body relaxes itself into losses. electric positivities
charge dragonfly wings beat red-white rd border outcomes
broadcasting: *what sort of border is this*? rds whining east at the
close to a crag. where a porter sits drawing on the edge of the
state. the pm issues a statement in condemnation of violence
& w/ violence retaliates. as families split on mountain's edge,
sharp as cameras spit & wage wars over borders' indecipherable
ciphers. in walkie talkies birds fly into electrified wire. the
sound of wind over walkies at crossings tossed into the fence.
btwn the tiny steel frame door a small concrete portal
& a stowaway

[a p p r o a c h i n g t h e b l a c k s e a]

for Rachel Blau DuPlessis

approaching the black sea hidden in light   & on
the other side of the sea   a valley whose height
they say reaches the sky   at what we shouted
be what may   so we began to walk on a slant through the
air across diagonal crevices   until we reached the
bottom what they said   where having felt the ground
          we stopped walking in the dark   instead a
cliff   of mountain air   & seeing that because of
steep smoothness   forced to clamber   with
hands & nails   teeth & tongues for sheer violent strength
to reach some top   & as soon as we stopped an
extraordinary silence: & there were many failed
believers there   seized by joy   & we did not
want to walk on the mountain with our whole bodies, saying
to ourselves: *we must protect ourselves*

[p o l a n d - p a l e s t i n e   l e t t e r]

for Ahmad Almallah

so that these words shall not be written to no-one   :
go ahead into the city of *al kuds*   what the ancestors called
jebus   & when you   come to the first gate
wait 9 weeks in meditation   fast,
                        & drink no water

& when we approached the first gate i remember   a bloody
larynx hung   at the threshold   a sign by which we shd
not go on   & by which you *cd* not
so that we swept our feet   across the entry-floor   as a sign to
the guards   we wd not leave

then in dusty corners of entry   we assembled
groups of students & teachers   poets & craftspeople
wherever &   whenever our words were exchanged
the first thoughts   we immediately grasped for

each after   the whole matter at hand from it
& from its meaning   as in
numerable keys popping up   in   thoughts as
words joined   up   & at last   we saw the first
            who also sat as teachers & students dressed-up like us
                        in *shatnez* coats

they immediately asked after   you   at which point
we have come   but have not the strength to say
what they asked   for   the ancestors who took that burden
on their backs   who packed themselves tightly in
                                        exile   tho dispersed

[c o n (d e) s t r u c t i o n]

for Gabriel Levin

in whatever shape or form it takes what breaks drills the
body wakes into "a land not promised you." on archipelagos
of sound, a silence rains, maimed & claimed as one of those
who knew you well. whomever sounds the sound resounds
& sorts the mounds & bodies left for dead. when the sun sets
over a different place. the place is not the place but the face,
she says. moment-to-moment, mouth-to-mouth, in the cave
of the shark in the body of a bird. i'm in bed by 10 a.m. with
my earplugs in & still the drilling persists. neurotic mists
conjure valleys of erotic shit - valleys of the wretched myth of
persistence. subsistence consists of existing conditions. a fist
in the shape of a rose. in the valley of resurrection. morning
re-covers strangled birds on all sides by blinding light we can't
see. it is the light before dark. it is the darkness probed in light.
if I am the site give me sight. to hold & behold, the cold not
the cold, our hunger not our hunger. w poems btwn our teeth,
feasting on the least & starving on the bones. in the beginning
we cut stone. in the beginning we roamed & combed ticks
from our sheep. sites & excursions excavate our lines. find &
do not find, in mine & not in mind. the yellow berries that
carried me thru sleep. corrupting my distracting by the wheat
of the week & saying we are those who have gone crazy. mark
yrself in ash above the temple. sort what cannot be sorted the
mortuaries mountains below above the summer snow. to know,
no, never to know, to go after what cannot be—

[sliced from the stairs &
 w/ all the stairs]

translated from the Hebrew of Avot Yeshurun

one day a door sliced the second-story
& the whole sand-loam-concrete floor rose & shifted & moved
& spilled & fled & was thrown from the stairs & w/ the stairs.
the room on the second story remained lit in the sun as before
in wood's supports naked
as before.

from whence was this taken?
from where does it derive?
what's it called?
what's it say?

[Note: These works, save the final translation, take place on the border of Israel/Palestine/Lebanon during two deep forensic architectural traverses I participated in, led by Riv Weinstock, & our Lebanese artist-architect-activist friend & collaborator, whose name we can't share for safety reasons, on the other side of the military fence. While Riv sketched, photographed, video & audio-recorded at various intersections along the naturalized war zone & border, I wrote these poems in response to the imposed silence of these sites, an eerie silence that I find radiates across the Syrian-African rift. On our second traverse, when we finally reached the border with Syria, we drove to Emek Ha-tsoakim *[The Shouting Valley], where an acoustic leak in the topography allows Druze families split across the divide to shout between countries in order to share news of their lives. The site has long been silent due to military intimidation. These poems attempt to tune-in to that acoustic leak, & to transmit some trace of a discontinuous echo across the arbitrary divide, a frequency otherwise erased by the sheer force & weight of the fence. Photographs in this section were taken by Riv Weinstock along the two traverses.-A.R.]*

LICK&SPIT:
TRANSINCANTATIONS

who	tricked	the	gods
into			collecting
impure	foods	to	infect
the	human		mouth
by			omen
everything			outside
which	does		not
c	o	m	e
b	a	c	k

LICK&SPIT//GODSOFNIGHT

      i call on you   gods of night
  estranged   from you   we became synthetic
to those   who knew you well   were unable to
fast   by day   at night
gaps continuously   fill our mouths
have kept yr food   now   far from lips   lessened
water passed throat   our praise-lament
who rejoices in mourning?   who stand by we
false gods   given heed   for grudge   & face
who grant decision
have forged a figure of our enchanter   "have lain in
fire"   brought   "the devil he did
against"   false as charges conjured
after rotted-body   earth but we shall live-out our   curses'
spells un-done   as the tamarisk   tall crown   who
chants   the date palm
chants   the maštakal makes
shine   fills the earth   in pine tree chants
  its seeds   confronted   by light
narden-grass   & smell of magic   words   falling
back into mouth   as rat-tongue tied up   you
gods of night   over
come in   three night-watches   dissolve
the spell our mouths   by talc
     our tongues by   salt

if a snake wraps around (a man)   let him go down
to the sea   & put a casket   over his head   & face
(the snake) opposite himself   &   when   (the
man) goes into (the casket)   let him lift (the
casket) into the water   & rise & consume 4 grains
of worm   (-colored) alkaline-plant   & wrap
it on his throat   or dress   or wind it   thru
coral   decocted ashen palms   roasted
then   smoothed-out   on its surface

L I C K & S P I T // I N W A R D M U R M U R

wind that carries   inward murmur   strikes   the
image   let
strike   what lies   let stand   for   false
gods let   speak the words of   warlock   fence
& qab-bu-ú witch: *šu'u-i-pa-áš-šar immeru i-pa-áš-šar*
the moles shall be free   --them be free!   their words may
be loosened   our word will   be " *pa-áš-šar* "
     (not to be loosed *a-mat a-qab-bu-ú a-mat-su-nu ana pân*
     the words we speak   their words cannot impede
                                        on the order of asalluhi
i false master of sound   our images
             my lords slanderers cursers   detract
-ors   lord nemeses   & who do you know them?
i don't know
them   tricks   fake magic   spells make
   evil plottings   incise   a pressure evil
cooker   turn hate   & fact-twisting murderers'
                                        mouths   take
                                                "change
of heart"   to glowing faces   as folly is
any   thing   they have   not yet   drawn   to
                                                              them

if   a   snake   is   tempted (by a man)   if
his 'charmer' is with   him   let (the
     'charmer') make him walk 4 miles   & if not   let
him cross 4   bridges   at night   place his head on 4 stones   &
sleep under   a moonless (sky)   or else bring   4 (feral)
cats   to tie them to the 4 rotted legs of   a sleeping
corpse   & make debris (of the body) so that   when   the
cats hear the (snake's) scream   they shall   devour him

LICK & S P I T // K N O T S U N D O N E

the magic we did   let it dissolve like salt
                         our knots undone   machinations
are all worlds   fill the steppe   on our
command   the gods of night
incant: o earth   yes earth   is the
master of yr curses
       what you have been we know   what you will
be   we do not yet   what yr scroll inscribes   is loose
& nobody else's   can undo   it has no
undoer but

incantation at zab-ban: my city zabban   my city

has two gates
to its east   i am lifting twd you   the bloom at
maštakal   to the gods of sky we bring water-

incantation to-end-all-countries: we have barred the
river-crossing   have barred the harbor
          held back the magic spells   to end-all-
countries   they have sent we   whom shall we send to
belit-seri   in the mouth of our warlock & witch
          thru incantation in the sage-god marduk   they
will call you   but do not answer
they will address you as object   but do not
submit
& only when they address you by force   only listen

       in order that   anu antu & belet-seri may hear
  but do not submit to force

incantation we-are-sent: we go   are ordered
we speak   against the wishes of the
warlock-witch asalluhi:
      beware yr surroundings   notice what is on this
earth   in yr country notice who speaks   & who
is spoken   what happened is still   happening

———————————————————————————

SNAKECHANT

```
if    a  snake  bites  (a  man)                          &  will  not  let
go                        if  the  venom  is  moving  thru  (them)
                          tie  the  wrist              &  if  not,  the  throat
      &  the remedy is                    they must  fornicate together
a human-reptile        (so there are those that say          what
will strengthen     (the snake's) inclination all the more) rather
    should they               take        burnt hair & toenails
&                     throw                    them                    (at
                               the      snake)      &      say,
```

from distress i, you servant lion of god   son of butcher
whose god   whose goddess is   *annannitumtum*
as-hur-ka   i have turned to you   having sought
you   (out
my hands are raised   at yr feet i throw   &
                                                          burn my
warlock-witch, šá   away my warlock-witch   lose
their lives   too fast   spared
my life   be
                                                          indebted

in cantation   de-   natured spell: w the help of an
icon in talcum   is the
meaning of yr name   who looks
licks darkness   as eternal
new-light   this country   writ false
          so licks all   things

  we who stand face you   restore muscle sinew   lick sins
                                        to šamaš   who
twist RIGHT
di-e-ni   *di-ni*   *purussâ-a-a purusus*
          so said
"restore the RIGHT" but   restoration makes
decision to yr ass-brat master   we are grabbing the crown
          at yr coat   yr rabbit ass-brat fur
                                                          restored

LICK & SPIT // KHURBNLIFE

those   who disposed of the bodies   executed in pits
yr neck they tied   yr back   they broke
drained blood from   cut muscle to sinew   yr
legs   they bound   with rope   & emptied
in spasm filling
let eat the cursed food let drink the cursed water   have
washed w dirty water &
smeared w
sour milk weed   have mocked   the living dead
     our khurbn life under
ground un marked   & you, fucking   girra
who burn the warlock-witch   who kill the wild offspring
destroy what is also you   who have called on   we   in
šamaš judge   who

                              will eat yr enemies
consume the ones who wish you evil   "may
they catch themselves cancer"   "may they find
their ends in sewers"   where we live   "may
their fingers like those of clumsy   masons"   crushed upon
yr   every false promise   which does not   waver

[Note: The poems in this suite (cor)respond to a group of ancient Akkadian exorcism incantations, several of which I first discovered in the form of Jewish-Aramaic adaptations in the Babylonian Talmud. I read the radical hybridity of the Talmudic discourse here as both precedent for, & invitation to, my own contemporary translinguistic praxis, one which engages writing as a mode of perpetual displacement—translating languages in wide spirals outward, to the farthest edges of the sonic/semantic divide—while gleaning materials for a poetics from even the most minute residues left behind. I've begun, in these terms, to compose & transpose from homophonic transliterations, as well as Aramaic & Hebrew translations of the Akkadian spells, stitching together poems from the translingual dregs between the gaps of the adapted texts.

The phrase, "Lick & Spit", I take from the Ashkenazi-Jewish folkloric expectoration ritual of licking a person's forehead three times, spitting between each lick—a physical gesture I associate most closely with the act of sucking venom from a snake bite—in order to exorcise the "evil eye" from the body. -A.R.]

DAYBOOKS

for jake

[l e v d a a s]

moses coincides w the people only forty years after (happy
birthday people!) we have attained the eyes to see, the ears
to hear, supposedly (but what does it mean, *lev daas*?) the
spectre in coded prepositions as polysemic as a credit card's
taxes or ids. it's symptomatic of mountain water peaks. the
chicken farmers buying-out the fan companies. for human
hair uses horse stiletto ashen porches, uses polish cinema
employees at the warsaw samsung factory. makes "all the
colors for all the kids." buys books. lifts bellies over rivers of
plants. machinations stands entities against anarchic waste.
stands identities against hearty software & "I solemnly swear"
vocabulary cards. justice fribourg dein schwein sonnen snout
dein swan remembering its former glory. from an alfred
aisenstaedt century, she reads, this time a-round, no tubing
in the tub down the danube. to which position is gegangen
"to the province of the self". & the belt of american media
corporations is the accordion of an ugly polka. companies
forgetting their function forget their names. ist di diagnostik
und adjusting it. the just dude in such circumstances must
approach the sprach error or will error sprach such yikhes will
error schreiben nor anschreiben error the many names now
erased

for charles

[f a l i y a h]

ascend description
the scripture the office
the alphabetic clear class cadillac XL scripture
the clear glass alphabetic eclairs clapping campion
adds stress to making campsites abstract
exits right index telling XM radio night jokes
abstracted exiles alphabetic
abstract ideological acoustics
is how the muse learned to write
index telic hesiod's ascend descriptors official alphabetic clear
class cadillac XL scripture the whole office clapping 'we are the
champions' exits right into
abstract ideo
logical acoustics is
how the muse
learned to write
in-dex tillich
axel meter

for kirk & zvi

[s h v a r i m (s h a t t e r i n g s)]

do you do you do you do you do you you you you

scoot off tectonic

sway moronic temp X 10

4 more caressing

less idly frightening live

inmate muster-board

basket money loaned

4 times less the term: in rows

a start me up forklift meter

whose lines elastic corn piping

hot flippies

or morbid bidding rides

5 bytes in 2 lines

motion in ear

repertoire force

in motion *be*

cause cats need water

more than *anything*

breaks mode iron glass glow

slow jam sandpaper specs

the slice of words looses hoops

& fixtures mixed tea

lick salt 6 licks textures

statues for change at the

mouthpeice bunker

sorted spelunker cork's

loose morphos matter

for alli

[a f i g]

we hire the best grade portion share order of something
sometimes as a saying equals my yr his her their thus "I didn't
get the joke" or often didn't get my always used before certain
often 'too' expected often too 'given' for me to me to stand
under the second connotation --

the sack zipped up up in order of a cup of coffee & bills &
orders a bowl of soup

at abe's cave gives $5 jukes uses rock & roll splicing techniques
since the first three squads or exceptionally fast hot-rod cars
w powerful or soupy motors cd be any atomic fucking bomb.
any plan or act that is so unusual as to be a fucking travesty
is something neither completely failed nor succeeding as
planned, nor expected, tho nearly

not a form of entertainment nor performance so dull or
inferior that it's called a travesty, cheap or inferior as an item of
poor design or quality when compared to the quote unquote
superior item

accidentally on purpose describes the willful actions so
carried-out to appear accidental or adventurously maliciously
sly at first used in vogue at frequent intervals since popular
sexual joculars came of age in $5 bills. of any person who
proved an outstanding gambler the first item in order of

importance is the ace not the whole, the person skilled in a
specific work, the specific fighter pilot shot down by at least
5 enemy planes. alright if it was 3 especially 3 but who gives
a tray or compartment of playing cards such high & low
numbers? containing extremes of high & lows only both right
& wrong answers at once can embody such contradictory
degrees

for erica

[s u k k o s]

plastic sizzles candle wrappers support wrapper plastics for
more sports eggs forks
more livers morgues live dialysis units manure corkages & de-
corkages jordily exhumed

exuberance exempted & corkages swelled to kvelling quits.
while failing at quietly bbqing the latest mince. the fourth
fortune skin-century dissection cuts from the first born

shows dynamic litter formerly "speech acts" shows dynamic
speaking from racist spokespersons
hate-addicts not dynamics attack the anonymous
beer factories.

shoshana citron margarita burns incense potpourri. smells
burnt smokey lemons. smells mint warped lemons.
west, past fresno

are citron myths my family? we are disoriented, finally

for schimmel

[l a w n s o n g]

leaves line crisp brown lawns notice trees down skeletal forms
cast lengthwise shadows.
cross sky's reflections buzzing cars in lawn mowers dusk the
dogs run in packs. part by park, part by sky's blue radical
compass. spanning space for places a language site or geo-
lingual host

might find. forced out words. pulled in words. side words
always to arrive not at the site.

tonite the birds disturb the dogs. the bears are dying in
their suits. daylight makes the night fast as fat as before. an
explosion in hinge from pterodactyl pupils. triangle pupils
quadrangle the radius. from above,
over & btwn the stems firm slants

for brandon

[l o s t l a n g u a g e s]

morning practice: walk before breakfast. fast before
fashionable: moths into light. ritual listening—fit split residual
reckoning: have you finished adjusting the fan belt band? it's
cooler today & my mood follows suite. light as feather & fluffy
as foam soothing our reunion in a poem.

& after all the friends have gone. & after the fire is only ash
& amber. one afternoon when the sun is beating hot & high.
you'll remember this humming breath how it was yrs

how it feels to sit even for a minute. the weight of faces
contracting in laughter. how many more here on this surface?
how many more here to these deeps? kept memories cracked
findings found lost languages behind us. it was our breaths
slow humming calling back

for ted

[s h p a t s i r n]

mirror memory glands unwrap round a harness fastened to
the middle of a busy street
course measured maximizing ursula's handprint in cement.
craving dry crayon coloring grass muted when marble lists
expectoration machinates mince-fish pies salvatation
transpires, still not fear
memory marks & cardstock sighs: matter, matter
yeah, yeah, holy blaspheming paraphrasing the rotting
nimrod statue.
whose forklift specials here half framed-out in print larceny &
penance: *don't anybody care about anybody*
any more?
pass me out facts makes smoldering s/mocks saturated teeth of
sensualized re(as)semblance --
festive popes half-the-time pruning & clippling
their holy nails.
who hear fishes at night & you catch the big one w/ a plow
breath(e) over the head of their picture - fetching the bait is
half the trip
eat yr supper - fresh fish.
reschedule this thing with the impossible in any monumental
sense but as a ghost limb
that street chorus' contusions elicit mystery illusory
holding patterns
in slow figure-eights serrate & break over recalcitrant tarmac

[Note: "Daybooks" comprises poems dedicated to other poets & artists, culled from my notebooks & daily writing praxes. If for Avot Yeshurun, poems are unsent letters to the dead, which he buries in the graves of his desk, I write these poems as wild love songs to my living friends, who make this life of poetry all the more livable & sweet. After we are all long gone, these poems will remain, I hope, as residues & records of our loving relations; or as my friend Schimmel likes to say: "my friends are never far, look, here they are, in their words."-A.R.]

AVOIDANCES

BIRD VALLEY

for ANF & LPI

the first time I heard the word
"jacuzzi"
in the German Colony Amazonian
parrots lined the telephon wires.
tessellated palm
fronds swayed
on
light & wind

GOLDEN CIRCLE

after the Yiddish of Avrom Sutskever

The clock stopped crying. The golden circle
is a hand closed in a hand.
Now you must measure with other measures:
Your doveheart in a mousetrap.

THE SPY

for Stephen Ross

At the grocery in Outremont
I listen to the men ahead of me in line
argue over a posek:
the laws of purification
for a woman.

It is summer;
the sabbath won't be in
until later,
but the grocery closes
the same time, every week.

"It has been this way for generations,"
reads the sign on the sliding door.
& the pale child pulling at his father's fringes,
asking—
tati, vus tut der goy in undzer grocery store?

KNEE-SHOT & THE WIDOW

on the 5th palms
the sabbath judge sits
in a field w/ the 2nd tulip -
if it's mine tulip to pine (says
the two lips of a judge pay
screwy lymph-nod service to
the knee-shot
widow on the 5th,
laughing "i'm me"
hey guy rough i mean
hagiography

WISDOM CHANGE

for Zali & Yorik

in or that
concealment of
un-concealment—

mind-numbing slides
we abided
by

total mudness

*

*Go thee then
as far as*

*thee can go
shall find*

*a thing
as close
as can be:*

*even Viennese
schnitzel*

*in
Kanyakumari . . .*

Only when
you go

you find
you cannot know

if you
are less-than
or more

-than
one.

    *

So what?! If the shit's human
           shit

it's not enough
           to say

it—you've gotta
           prove it.

The clock-safe ticks
           only after

inserting the coin
           you can wind.

FROM MANNEQUINS

after the Yiddish of Dvoyre Fogel

Sorrowfulnesses are a decorative element of life

all life can become decorative; this happens when a raw heroic schema, to which the fullness of life gets reduced, unmasks the ur-schema of monotony.

One must return then to interpretation (to "the superstructure") of the few raw facts of life.

Like an ornament, the life-zone thus gets filled with events: an ornament of events that doesn't leave a spare drop of room for monotony.

The raw, concentrated, three-dimensional life-clump here becomes like a two-dimensional one. Superficial decoration.

But with the decorativistic (de)composition of life without any event remainder — there awakens a psychic constellation of reckoning with somewhere existent, ready-made things: things that "need to come," and the only possible state: of waiting; the awaiting of ready-made possibilities. From "experiences" which can come or not come.

DEFORMINGLIGHTS: HEBRAICINFLECTION

for (J)ML & (S)JR

maybe

although

friends

crown   kosherly   fringed
prayer-shawls,   leather straps,   *shulkhan-*
orekh,   *zohar*   world-to-come purposes

fashioned after

contradict

moon

friend

content   friend

guilty

envy   expert,   cousin

friend

content

repeat

exile,

complaints.

Galilee. . .

void   "alef"   "sof".

truth

truth   friend

while

                                                friend

                            error

     truth

     So be it!

chasm   particular.

   truly   doubt

             sway   peacefully --

                      friend,

              Galilee

                 friend

    hereafter

                     in relation to --

DEFORMINGLIGHTS:
SLAVICINFLECTION

for (J)ML & (S)JR

stately,

though

though

artillery

stately,   gauntlet,
                              lash.

                                               panting
                                                curiosity:

                                                              nu?

stately

buzzes

stately

[Note: "Deforming Lights" is a cross-inflectional erasure influenced by Lisa Samuel's & Jerome McGann's isolational deformance procedures & based on Mikhl Likht's "Every New Poet," which I translated from the Yiddish in collaboration with Stephen Ross. To create these multilingual deformances, I went through Likht's "Every New Poet" and color-coded the Hebraic and Slavic inflections; I then "whited-out" all but the Hebraic registers (in the first variation) and all but the Slavic registers (in the second). The micro-inflectional textures these deformances reveal—in the form of erasure's "relief"—ripple across Likht's writing & provide us rich tonal information that we wd not otherwise receive from a standard (monolingual) close reading of his work. These poems then - these "deformed" translations - also serve as critical research materials within the emerging fields of translingual & expanded-Yiddish poetics.-A.R.]

NOT FROM MEMORY

for Jennifer Bartlett

Wasps & bees banned together
(meanwhile
without permission
of the birds

to state the obvious:

at the Borsalino Hat Store in Bnai Brak
the man at the counter asks
after my accent:

nu, vus bistu, chabad?

Not me.
At least

not from
memory
tho
before
around
over
after
again.

Not from   any   where   but
    body   knuckle   bone

non-mind

idiom of
sound

Y I N G L O S S I A
S T U D I E S : 1 - 5

to escape the perpetual torments inflicted upon it,
the dybbuk-tongue seeks refuge in a garbled mouth...

(1)

My chronic itch
may it bring health upon our navel
for small favors
w/ minor fortunes
& big doings --
THE REAL DEAL:
a-thenticity
I don't give a hang about.
To all those happy-go-lucky people,
they should live!
What a few chews wdn't do
after midnight
when the hostess serves
peanut hor d'ouvres.
As long as a lung
or liver hangs
on the nose
another disease made
easier to stomach
rash on my ass
made less to bare

Maw to the ear might
serve me right
for a year & a Wednesday
a slice of gan eden.
Healthful as a body
can be (under the
circumstances.
Tho it shdn't happen
to the worst of us
(cd be said about
any of us. Too smart to do it
ourselves
in spite of everything that
churns out wrong.
Culturally impudent finicky bagatelle.
Getting senile?
Find some absented-mind
-ed peace already.
An alphabet for
alphabet
's first language
jitters. & to all those
cobblers
walking barefoot
thru the streets
give them shoes!
Not the one & just
-born excuse
in over-dressed wandering.

Majority rules. Minority's
a joke.

Really? That's
how it goes?
That's what they said

(2)

Concealed in
bobby-yarns
inventing lift-off
praise
for rolls w/ holes. Burying
our names
fledged no easy feat.
"Teamsters!"
they screamed

(the respectable chews,
"waggoneers,
"coachmen! dis-honorable
"faith-healer
"gossips
"drummed-up
"for a baron taboo
"fornicated
"for the fun of it!"

"So don't screw
"me around," slashing out
the show-pup rebbe
spoke:

"You there, in a hurry
"standing on one leg
"over an egg:
"what are you, nuts?
"While white-cheese pancakes
"puff hot pride
"over bobby-yarn!"
(small things, pea
-nut holdovers,
the price of a hotel
room in the Catskills.

Still fond of
borsht botshvine
brunches
chronic stomach
aches made brave.

(3)

after Lucretius

but there's nuthin more delightfillt
like to live in that zalm well as
the teachings of the wise temples teach

you can look down on others & see
to fumble & wander here & there to seek the ways in life
able to fight, worldly
night & day with the help of hard work
to the top of the peak of cash & power.
how crooked are the minds of people's blind chests!
those in darkness, how great the dangers of life
to come that pass the time! those we don't see
are just the nature of the bark, but to those who
the body means pain, god forbid, it should take the mind from
our delightfillt sense of *shpilkes*.
(4)

after Ralph Waldo Emerson

Persist fer yerself, never impersonate. Yer own talent you can
hide every side with the growin craft from that whole lotta
livin; only from the learnt talent of somebody else, do you get
such an ad lib fifty/fifty estate-trade. So what's everybody doin
better? Nothin! As tho a big shot swindler had learnt them.
Nobody knows what's what, or even can know it, till he's done
it. What boss learnt Shakespeare? & what boss, Franklin?
Or Washington? Bacon? Newton? Every big shot is his own
particular. The Scipionism from Scipio is, im tellin ya, like a
dumpling that can't be split. Shakespeare could never be learnt
thru Shakespeare. Make like what's expected, & don't bother
hopin too much, or convokin too much, neither. It's in the
moment, dontcha see? A chatterbox heroics & big-shot sound,
like it was from that grand ham Phidias, or that ancient
Egyptian trouble, or your old uncle Moyshe, or even Mr. D.d.

Alighieri, but still, differently. No afternoon snack will the
loaded soul, all fluid, even with a thousand glowing tongues,
give a do-over; only if you listen-in to what the fathers hum,
then be my guest, & answer them in that same vocal grade;
since the ear & the tongue are two organs from one nature.
Stick around in the straightforward genteel neighborhoods
of life, mind your gut, that you should replicate the old world
anew.

(5)

after Claudia Rankine

a friend tyin it as American or shlock: "it's fishin the historyish,
as I think (I think. Let them see middle-ear immersed inter-
act. we friends meet, get inside the rove-tail. compatible
personality test over mole historyish self. ear-white, as I think
I'm dyin, she's far seethe odor dyin, white seethe in ear, as far's
I think. oncomin meets w/ full craft fume dyin, "American"
or "positionin." them old ear scent she ties & digs, punnin to
punnin in second, as was fishin the libel left smiles, wrecked
fume dyin miles. or was hot ear soakin. instantaneously dyin
attachment meant swath tenuous under, to cane a veda fume
dyin, as I think. in coach dyin, I guess ribbon personless
history, as zen gem meant to rat oven cautious ear fume.
misunderstandin they use chivalry, grunt ear to ear, stain of
earth. going soon to what was (is) meant.

[Note: The title of this cycle, A V O I D A N C E S, has multiple connotations across English-Yinglish-Yiddish-&-Hebrew. In English, (a)voiding solidity, against conclusion or paraphrase; presenting meaning which does not close-in on itself but opens outward onto multiple absences; the void dance of never settling on both feet at once. In a legacy of nomadic poetry, both modern Jewish & pre-islamic Qasida, which is always on the move by process of encircling. In Hebrew "Avoda"; in Yinglish & Yiddish, "Avoyde": understood in modern terms as "work" either in the external world or on the internal self; in the ancient context, Avo(y)da as sacrifice, a ceremony of giving way to something. Also associated with "avo(y)da zara" or idol worship: sacrifice to the wrong source. -A.R.]

CODA:
EVERY NEW POET

CODA :
"EVERYNEWPOET: PROEM"

After the Yiddish of Mikhl Likht[1]

My luck: I want to find the sublime, stately, sober words and
fasten them to my own, imagined, rapt ones -- maybe I will
successfully reflect life -- Jewish life[2], in
particular:
although art has nothing to do with life, against all
anachronisms, not respecting Shakespeare's pathetic and
bathetic Burshteinisms[3] (by my worthy friends the stamps
"talent" and "graphomania" lie half-dusty in little boxes). --
Already from the rips in the web, the contradictions. The first
bite, hard to swallow, are the imagined words. Against, they
stand -- (with golden *ateyros*[4] and kosherly braided *tsitses*[5])
in old silk *taleysim*[6], wrapped in *retsues*[7], *shulkhn-orekh'd*[8],
zoyer'd[9] with *oylem hobe*[10]

1 Translated in collaboration with Stephen Ross.
2 "Yiddish lebn" can mean both "Jewish" and "Yiddish" life,
and Likht is playing with the ambiguity.
3 Pesach Burstein (1896 - 1986) - Jewish-American comedian, singer,
songwriter, and director of Yiddish vaudeville theater.
4 Yiddish (from Hebrew): pl. "crown."
5 Yiddish (from Hebrew): "knotted ritual fringes worn by observant Jews."
6 Yiddish (from Hebrew): pl. "Jewish prayer shawl."
7 Yiddish (from Hebrew): pl. "phylactery straps."
8 Neologism using the name of the Jewish legal code book, *Shulkhan Arukh*.
9 Neologism using the name of the mystical Hebrew text, *Zohar*; puns on the
Yiddish word for "sour" (*zoyer*).
10 Yiddish (from Hebrew): "the world to come."

purposes, the dictionary words. They *shokl*[11] themselves
methodically in alphabetically sorted rows over our head-hair
like fruit-trees, ripe.

And I want to be fashioned after nature and create the
regimentation of language that would make a new order in
human knowledge. How, heaven forbid, is an apple more
poetic, though not more meaningful, when rhymed with a
krepl[12] than that which doesn't rhyme in sound but is only
formed in the *nepl*[13] of characteristic order? And how much
sin against words that, graphologically, contradict themselves,
though they are wholly and thoroughly philological?

"Flesh and stone and gold and fine buildings" are more the
motif of enthusiastic growth in human language than sun and
moon and stars. A friend, a versifier. A reader of mine (fictive,
of course) reads my stuff. I have the last word -- so he assumes:
written, he believes, it is lost. He does not know that after
publication, black on white, of my own words, the imaginary
ones, they haze the native-words away from the places, the
highly-esteemed ones, and set up, in a certain sense, in lines
(according to human knowledge) they begin to shoot with
cannons and artillery from their contents.

---

11 Yiddish: "to shake or tremble", used to describe the traditional Jewish prayer
motion.
12 Yiddish: "dumpling"; also, an interlingual pun on "crap."
13 Yiddish: "fog," continuing the rhyme.

My friend, a reader etc., stands from afar and takes great pleasure: his words, the stately, the sublime ones, accompany, run my gauntlet, whip their skin off with an *al-khet*[14] lash. The critique, he says choking himself on rivalrous gall, the critique is an expert, a cousin to that which is. The critique, another friend continues with his kind disposition, is a corrupted "that" which doesn't know who pulled the wool over its eyes (the friend -- one who is idiosyncratic, neologistic, wakes up panting).

But, Jewish life? The content of art? Huh? Listen to this curiosity: once was a people, a land. . . but is there any value in repeating that which history translated into *goles*,[15] into need, into shameful shudders, into poisonous complaints, into begged bread? "*Nu*, there once was in my land, the green land in the hilly corner of the Galilee. . . with thirty silver pieces".[16] The three-pointed void locks in the story from "*alef*" to "*sof*".[17] "The burglary that already happened": Is this the good news that cleaves the people to their children? -- "I was sent to you by God": Does this mean, in a sense, a truth exchanged through a lie? A bare truth through a gilded lie?

14 "On the transgression…", prayer of confession recited on Yom Kippur while beating one's chest.
15 Yiddish (from Hebrew): "Exile."
16 The amount Judas was paid to betray Jesus, Matthew 27:3-10.
17 "From A to Z."

Art, says my friend (the former, not the latter) art must defeat
one's own words the thoughtful ones.[18] Art, he says, is the "I
won't be late in life," but while here I won't play with it,
only grab at life's coat-tails,[19] to provoke, to rouse, so it can,
for the sake of tone, bend Newton's established laws (with
"established" ones my friend makes an error!); Zeno will
philosophize out the truths that I desire: my spirit will befriend
all those deep, sharp, sublime, and stately words. --

So be it! I will barely succeed at reflecting life -- the *thom*[20]
of Jewish life in particular. Art has absolutely nothing to do
with life: life means the table on which I am writing now; the
fly that buzzes around my head incessantly; through the little
window inward-shining sun (fuller than two others, according
to the tradition of sublime, stately word-mixtures: she really
sets?[21] what does she see? I doubt it); a man from the other
side[22] of the pane who rolls by in an imagined thing; the dust;
the trees that *shokl* like a person praying peacefully -- the trees
in the church square.

18 *Farklerte* (slant rhymes with *verter*): perhaps a reference to Schoenberg's
"Verklärte Nacht" (1899). This sentence is notably sing-songy.
19 *"...raysn s'lebn bay di poles"*, punning on the English "riding by the coat-tails."
20 Yiddish (from Hebrew): "depths, abyss, chasm"—a word with strong biblical
resonances (cf. Genesis 1:1).
21 Set: Likht is punning on the Yiddish for both "full" and "to see," in addition
to the English "setting sun."
22 Double entendre on "the world to come."

But none of this is true.

No table, sun, person, fly, trees, machinery, no church
square; but yes, there exist words stately that lull my friend,
-- words sublime way before the music of "The Burglary that
Happened," or "...was once a land -- in the Galilee...with thirty
silver pieces," long long before "flesh and stone and gold and
fine buildings". Thus my luck improves: I found my way to the
dictionary and

fastened the sublime, stately words together with my own
imagined ones, taboo.
And my friend, a reader etc, will link them hereafter[23]
with favorable or unfavorable critique, and consider them in
relation to --
with love or gall -- life and art.

[Adam Kadmon]

1

Held in the ancient footlights of time --
A shake: and they fall like apples from trees
the *klipos*[24] that trace a circular chain
in loud-umlaut . . . klezmer, as they say,

23 "*Lehabe*": a reference to "*oylem hobe*," the world to come in rabbinic Judaism.
24 Yiddish (from Hebrew): Shells; also demons.

testing fiddles and woodwinds;
the noisy interweaving -- a *gilgul*[25] of tones
like a symphony of decadents;
But perhaps Bach or Byrd became wholly the one

who receives the elevation and overs[26] the hour
that grows from minutes to eternity? . . .
. . . the *klipos* clatter the chain around *nefesh*[27]
with demonic calm: devour! devour!

And *klipos* in *gilgul* from over -- glug-glug:
the first eleven *oysyes*[28] from A' to K'
with *sfiros*[29] multiplied from one (1) to zero (0),
and *summa summarum*[30] -- from L' to Z'.

25 Yiddish (from Hebrew): Transformation; metamorphosis.
26 *Avor't*: from Hebrew (to pass).
27 Yiddish (from Hebrew): Soul.
28 Yiddish (from Hebrew): Letters.
29 Yiddish (from Hebrew): Kabbalistic term for mystical emanations of the Divine.
30 Latin: "On the whole; all in all."

UNNATURALBIRDMIGRATOR

as wild turkeys eat from the "bread of nights"
so must we eat from the "bread called sky"
we are not even this

must we wear a hat of degradation
in contempt for
the split

across skin thin borders
btwn "i" & my
nest.

but we have already eaten from
the crazy wheat
(called sky

knowing from the
first moment of
knowing we cannot stabilize

either side. a split that has
no story—
you cannot tell

in the saf—safa

d o o r s w a y o f l a n g u a g e

a loose-lipped Moses
stutterering himself
for hiccupping Aristophones

in an ocean of words
coming up to see the view *<the fable of the fish>*
"planet earth has a very strong smell"
    the birds repeat—

ACKNOWLEDGMENTS

I want to acknowledge my ancestors, grandparents & parents, who gifted me multifarious tongues through sidelong diasporic pasts—paths to my polyglot present & future; & my poet/artist kith, spread across languages & geographies, in ongoing conversation, who animate & co-populate this work. I'm grateful, in particular, to Ted Rees, Alli Warren, Sara Larsen, Brandon Brown, Lewis Freedman, Steve Seidenberg, Julia Warner, Stephen Ross, Jason Mitchell, Kristen Gallagher, Ahmad Almallah, Chris Alexander, Rachel Blau DuPlessis & Louis Chude-Sokei for their love & care in this life of writing & through it all.

With very special thanks to Will Alexander, Charles Bernstein, Maria Damon, Adeena Karasick, erica kaufman & Tyrone Williams for their extremely generous readings & responses to the book; & an overflowing thank you to Pierre Joris for his ecstatic nomadic preface; with love & thanks to Elæ, for their guidance, support and friendship over the many years, & for believing in this book & seeing it into the world; & the whole Operating System organismo: I love ya'll, thank you for everything you make happen. & finally, the most enormous thank you to Riv Weinstock, for designing this book & for being my #1 person, partner, collaborator & co-parent *biz eybik* & beyond. Zamir Shalom will discover this book some day soon & when he does we'll show him, *look, Ima & Aba made this.*

I wish to also thank the editors of *Golden Handcuffs Review*, *Jacket2*, *Dibur Journal*, *The Wolf Magazine for Poetry*, *Wave Composition*, *Global Modernists on Modernism*, *X-Peri* and *Tinge Magazine* for publishing many of the poems and translations included in this book. Thank you to Jerry Rothenberg for publishing "Membrane Chant" in the 3rd edition of *Technicians of the Sacred*. Thanks, also, to Norbert Lange and Norbert Wehr for publishing Sonja vom Brocke's German translation of "Yinglossia" in *Schreibheft, Zeitschrift für Literatur #93*. Photographs in "third space" are by Riv Weinstock. Cover Image is Michael Sgan-Cohen's קן לציפור, כן לציפור, דרור לציפור, *Unnatural Bird Migrator*, Silkscreen & Acrylic on paper, 1983, (c) Courtesy of the Artist's Estate.

ABOUT THE AUTHOR

*photo: Riv Weinstock*

ARIEL RESNIKOFF is a poet, scholar, translator, editor and educator. With Stephen Ross, he is at work on the first critical bilingual edition of Mikhl Likht's modernist Yiddish long poem, Processions, and with Lilach Lachman and Gabriel Levin, he is translating into English the collected writings of the translingual-Hebrew poet, Avot Yeshurun. He has taught courses on multilingual diasporic literatures at the Center for Programs in Contemporary Writing (UPenn) and at BINA: The Jewish Movement for Social Change. In 2019, he completed his PhD in Comparative Literature and Literary Theory at the University of Pennsylvania, and he is currently a Fulbright Postdoctoral US Scholar. Ariel lives with his partner the artist and designer, Riv Weinstock and their toddler, Zamir Shalom, in Alameda, California, on unceded Ohlone territory. They will soon be departing for a 2-year stay in the Judaean Mountains / Jibal al-Khalil.

EXPERIMENTAL ANTIBODIES FOR WHATEVER THE ONGOING CATASTROPHE OF THIS LIFE DEMANDS

[An OS Conversation with Ariel Resnikoff]

Greetings! Thank you for talking to us about your process today! Can you introduce yourself, in a way that you would choose?

Ariel Resnikoff: failed-sabbatean rag peddler, cellar dweller, basement encased erasure maker, place displacer, language tracer, translator-poet-cipher, unnaturalbirdmigrator, odd carbon slew, troubled troubling jew.

Why are you a poet/writer/artist?

To translate the languages of my dreams, I became a poet. To translate the languages of my ancestors' dreams, I became a translator. Making art for me - in whatever form - is a means & a need, an infinite combination of strategies to survive through the contemporal violent darkness that surrounds. It is a light to look at, as much as to see & read by. A light to lighten the load, the trauma of history buried in our bodies. Or to shift it, at least, from back to shoulder, from right to left leg, hip to hip. To transfer the ever heavier weight of our outer & inner shitstorms & somehow carry on, to get through to the other side of whatever, to survive in writing, in translation, despite it all.

When did you decide you were a poet/writer/artist (and/or: do you feel comfortable calling yourself a   poet/writer/artist, what other titles or affiliations do you prefer/feel are more accurate)?

To speak to what I wrote above: the first time I dreamed in poems, I was living in a tiny isolated village called Yarnton, about 6 miles from the University of Oxford. Everything about Oxford & Oxfordshire made me feel hyper-Jewish & hyper-American, more Jewish & more American than I had ever felt before or have ever felt since. & my English felt constantly re/strained in relation to that grand standardizing English institution.

I remember when they matriculated (I almost wrote *inoculated*!) me into the university one Saturday afternoon in a stagnant Latin pomp & ceremony, I ran to a friend's place afterward to eat some cholent (traditional Jewish sabbath stew) to warm myself from the horrid chill of the Anglo Empire's ugly breath. To cut through the Anglo-Latinate static of that place, I would read & recite & listen to recordings of Yiddish modernist poetry constantly: Yankev Glatshteyn, Celia Dropkin, Avrom Sutzkever, Rokhl Korn, Dovid Hofshteyn, Kadya Molodowsky, Anna Margolin, Mikhl Likht. One night, in the cold dark of winter, I dreamed a Yiddish poem, though whose it was I did not know. My own? But I didn't recognize it. I awoke in the dead of night & went to my desk, turned on the lamp & began translating whatever I could remember. This went on for many nights, for several weeks, through the heart of the harshest winter of my life. When I finally began to dream in English again I had been changed into a poet & a translator.

What's a "poet" (or "writer" or "artist") anyway? What do you see as your cultural and social role (in the literary / artistic / creative community and beyond)?

Avot Yeshurun writes: "Perhaps not every person is a prophet. But every person is a poet. Because poetry obliges that a person respond to everything." This is one way into talking about my poethics & sense of poetic denizenship on one foot. Ultimately, being a poet & translator is, for me, about a human responsibility to biological & cosmological life, & the critical human ability to respond to that life—as Terrence Des Pres puts it in his *Survivor*—& to whatever the ongoing catastrophe of that life demands. Perhaps it is also, as Isaac Bashevis Singer suggested in his Nobel Prize speech, about preparing oneself & one's world for an afterlife yet to come; that is, about preparing in this world for a better world beyond, which we must nevertheless find ways to imagine & build toward in the here & now. This is not to say that this work necessarily succeeds or is ever complete (in fact it rarely does & never is), but I tend to think of my role as the Talmud holds: "Do not be daunted by the enormity of the world's grief. Do justly now, love mercy now, walk humbly now. You are not obligated to complete the work, but neither are you free to abandon it." I especially love the Talmud as a model & precedent here, since it responds to this grief in every manner possible - polymodal to the max - in intricate transtemporal discourses, conversations, commentaries, glosses, translations, narratives, anecdotes, proverbs, meditations, lists, gossip, ramblings, scramblings, diasporic glyphs, & always, notably, with necessary humor & radical ongoing openness.

Talk about the process or instinct to move these poems (or your work in general) as independent entities into a body of work. How and why did this happen? Have you had this intention for a while? What encouraged and/or confounded this (or a book, in general) coming together? Was it a struggle?

These works became a manuscript one night when I printed out ninety-or-so pages of them at the print shop at 39th & Walnut in West Philadelphia & took them back to our drafty apartment on Springfield Ave & laid the pages out on the wide hardwood floor of our bedroom & began arranging them—like keys of a piano, I was thinking at the time. When Riv got home from the studio around 2AM, she was surprised (but let's be honest, also *not that* surprised) to find me splayed out on the floor scuffling around with my papers, Duke Ellington's *Money Jungle* playing loudly on the stereo. But there it was: *Unnatural Bird Migrator* arrived in the world that night, on the cold smooth floor under Ellington's "Solitude" (Charles Mingus on bass, Max Roach on drums) in a sea of shuffling texts.

Did you envision this collection as a collection or understand your process as writing or making specifically around a theme while the poems themselves were being written / the work was being made? How or how not?

I like to think that this collection operates sort of like a 'choose your own adventure' to translingual poetry. There are so many ways into it—as my elder Reznikoff liked to say, you can open at any page & read away—& just as many ways out. The organizational mechanism has everything to do with the very particular ways in which I work, in the most banal & everyday, but also in the most existential of senses. That is, that every poem begins for me as an act of translation from an/other—call it ghost—language, & every act of translation is therefore ultimately infused with a translingual poetics. I think of myself as a translational contact tracer, in these terms, if language is indeed a virus as Bill Burroughs held; & I aim in my work to track down the transgressive dynamics of intermingled & intermingling tongues. This collection hopes to engage the reader, not merely as a spectator, but as an active collaborator in that search.

What formal structures or other constrictive practices (if any) do you use in the creation of your work? Have certain teachers or instructive environments, or readings/writings/work of other creative people informed the way you work/write?

I work with dozens of dictionaries & lexicons across multiple languages, a habit I picked up as a Yiddish & Hebrew translator. I also often cultivate numerous versions of a work in many different languages & forms, before finally hosting the poem as a translation in English words, though not always. Just recently, for example, I translated a poem of Charles Bernstein's *into* Yiddish; & Jerome Rothenberg & I have a collaboration that crosses between Yiddish & English with no "original" in sight.

Many many teachers & comrades across languages & geographies have helped to raise & shape me as a writer over the years. But perhaps I'll just admit here that the first innovative poetry & poetics I encountered was not in fact of an English strain at all, but in Yiddish, in the works of the Introspectivist writers who called themselves *Inzikh* (in-oneself). These New York Yiddish modernists of the first-half of the twentieth-century were pushing the boundaries of their language as far as—& in certain cases much further than—the high Anglo-modernists on the other side of the language divide. They were writing, however, in a language already projected into extinction by antisemites & statist Jews alike, which never actually died altogether, but which was translated outward, in a disappearing act that led to vast & uncharted variegated afterlives in other languages. These translingual afterlives arise as latent sparks in my own poetry & translation, flickering across every page as I transinscribe my work into writing.

Speaking of monikers, what does your title represent? How was it generated? Talk about the way you titled the book, and how your process of naming influences you and/or colors your work specifically.

The book takes its title from Michael Sgan-Cohen's silkscreen & acrylic on paper, *Unnatural Bird Migrator*, which he gifted to the poet, Zali Gurevitch, after showing the black-&-white (just silkscreen) version at the Tel Aviv Museum of Art. It hangs on Zali's wall & I have always been extremely taken by it, & by its ancestor, the 14th-century Birds' Head Haggadah; & somehow, without my realizing exactly, it became the guiding image of the collection & ultimately, also, the cover of the book.

I recently wrote Gurevitch to ask for his *drash* on the artwork, since it sits in his house & Michael was one of his closest friends. His response:

"Michael turns the bird into a metaphor for the mind or the soul that dwells in the head of the jewish migratory bird. So *ken* (nest) is written as *ken* (yes). It now means - say yes to the bird, like yes we can, or say yes to flying, wandering, imagining, which is further emphasized by *dror* (liberation, freedom) to the bird, with a rhyme – *dror la tzipor*. The drawing that Michael added to the specific print and the citation (Deuteronomy 33:2) brings into the picture the exodus of the children of israel in the desert, which reverberates the jewish story of liberation with that of any individual whose bird is caged in their head."

What does this particular work represent to you as indicative of your method/creative practice? your history? your mission, intentions, hopes, plans?

Unnatural Bird Migrator presents a radical translingual praxis at its outer edges, worn at the corner of any given language tapestry disguised as a common rag. It takes the human body as a model for a living archive of history, which stores everything & anything, all life's banal particulars, spoken or unspoken or misspoken or broken or defective or abnormal. The translingual strains this book channels into the viral host of English might also be understood as experimental antibodies, or as healing totems—or we might say *totafot*, in Hannah Weiner's sense—in perpetual resistance to the ongoing violence of an imposed silence within any national language system.

What does this book DO (as much as what it says or contains)?

UNBM aims to shift the tectonic ambiences that surround us in our everyday language(d) lives: to shimmer, to slide across the eye, to stumble, startle & in some cases even sting the tongue, while still tantalizing & dancing with it, to shake the ears awake.

What would be the best possible outcome for this book? What might it do in the world, and how will its presence as an object facilitate your creative role in your community and beyond? What are your hopes for this book, and for your practice?

The best possible outcome would be for someone to read what's held in these pages. More than perfect, in the Emersonian sense, would be for someone to respond to this work in writing, translation, or otherwise, to expand on it, to take it further & make it their own in whatever way. If I can elicit response to my work, which is itself a response to the world of languages I live in, if I can elicit a chain of witness to & through this book, I have fulfilled my poethic responsibility, I hope; & even if I elicit no response, as the Talmud says, I must at least make an attempt.

Let's talk a little bit about the role of poetics and creative community in social and political activism, so present in our daily lives as we face the often sobering, sometimes dangerous realities of the Capitalocene. How does your process, practice, or work otherwise interface with these conditions?

If nothing else, I hope this work disrupts business as usual; I hope it clogs the gears in the language machinery of the police state & general state of things. This work insists, above all, on the existence of subterranean translingual landless counterstates—as radically powerful as they are officially powerless—that survive in perpetual hiding beneath the iron thumb of the (language) police. Remembering always Kafka's nightmare of interpolation in *The Trial*, this book responds to the sadistic death call of the cops, licking & spitting away the evil eye of their shiny badges as a combination prayer-curse: MAY THEY BE DISARMED & DEFUNDED IMMEDIATELY UNTIL THE END OF TIME.

I'd be curious to hear some of your thoughts on the challenges we face in speaking and publishing across lines of race, age, ability, class, privilege, social/cultural background, gender, sexuality (and other identifiers) within the community as well as creating and maintaining safe spaces, vs. the dangers of remaining and producing in isolated "silos" and/or disciplinary and/or institutional bounds?

As artists & organizers, we need to not only tear down the gates & disarm & defund the gatekeepers, but also, to search out those that have been unjustly disenfranchised for whatever reason & by whatever means, & invite them in to reshape the existing conversation & culture as it stands. *Nu*, invite them in, I hear my grandmother say: into our landless diaspora of poetic/aesthetic influence & lineage; & let us share in the powerful treasures & traditions of our powerlessnesses. "How wide our arms"— indeed, thinking of Zukofsky's translation of Yehoash—a myriad on myriad must we seek & be.

Is there anything else we should have asked, or that you want to share?

For audio & video recordings of my work in the expanded poetic field, please visit my PennSound page:

http://writing.upenn.edu/pennsound/x/Resnikoff.php

ABOUT GLOSSARIUM:UNSILENCED TEXTS

The Operating System's GLOSSARIUM: UNSILENCED TEXTS series was established in early 2016 in an effort to recover silenced voices outside and beyond the canon, seeking out and publishing contemporary translations, translingual projects, and little or un-known out of print texts, in particular those under siege by restrictive regimes and silencing practices in their home (or adoptive) countries. We are committed to producing dual-language versions whenever possible.

Few, even avid readers, are aware of the startling statistic reporting that less than three percent of all books published in the United States, per UNESCO, are works in translation. Less than one percent of these (closer to 0.7%) are works of poetry and fiction. You can imagine that even less of these are experimental or radical works, in particular those from countries in conflict with the US or where funding is hard to come by.

Other countries are far, far ahead of us in reading and promoting international literature, a trend we should be both aware of and concerned about—how does it come to pass that attentions in the US become so myopic, and as a result, so under-informed? We see the publication of translations, especially in volume, to be a vital and necessary act for all publishers to require of themselves in the service of a more humane, globally aware, world. By publishing 7 titles in 2019, we raised the number of translated books of literature published in the US that year *by a full percent*. We plan to continue this growth as much as possible.

The dual-language and translingual titles either in active circulation or forthcoming in this series include Arabic-English, Farsi-English, Polish-English, French-English, Faroese-English, German-English, Danish-English, Yaqui Indigenous American translations, Yiddish-English and Spanish-English translations from Cuba, Argentina, Mexico, Uruguay, Bolivia, and Puerto Rico.

The term 'Glossarium' derives from latin/greek and is defined as 'a collection of glosses or explanations of words, especially of words not in general use, as those of a dialect, locality or an art or science, or of particular words used by an old or a foreign author.' The series is curated by OS Founder and Creative Director Elæ with the help of global collaborators and friends.

The Operating System uses the language "print document" to differentiate from the book-object as part of our mission to distinguish the act of documentation-in-book-FORM from the act of publishing as a backwards-facing replication of the book's agentive *role* as it may have appeared the last several centuries of its history. Ultimately, I approach the book as TECHNOLOGY: one of a variety of printed documents (in this case, bound) that humans have invented and in turn used to archive and disseminate ideas, beliefs, stories, and other evidence of production.

Ownership and use of printing presses and access to (or restriction of printed materials) has long been a site of struggle, related in many ways to revolutionary activity and the fight for civil rights and free speech all over the world. While (in many countries) the contemporary quotidian landscape has indeed drastically shifted in its access to platforms for sharing information and in the widespread ability to "publish" digitally, even with extremely limited resources, the importance of publication on physical media has not diminished. In fact, this may be the most critical time in recent history for activist groups, artists, and others to insist upon learning, establishing, and encouraging personal and community documentation practices. Hear me out.

With The OS's print endeavors I wanted to open up a conversation about this: the ultimately radical, transgressive act of creating PRINT /DOCUMENTATION in the digital age. It's a question of the archive, and of history: who gets to tell the story, and what evidence of our life, our behaviors, our experiences are we leaving behind? We can know little to nothing about the future into which we're leaving an unprecedentedly digital document trail — but we can be assured that publications, government agencies, museums, schools, and other institutional powers that be will continue to leave BOTH a digital and print version of their production for the official record. Will we?

As a (rogue) anthropologist and long time academic, I can easily pull up many accounts about how lives, behaviors, experiences — how THE STORY of a time or place — was pieced together using the deep study of correspondence, notebooks, and other physical documents which are no longer the norm in many lives and practices. As we move our creative behaviors towards digital note taking, and even audio and video, what can we predict about future technology that is in any way assuring that our stories will be accurately told – or told at all? How will we leave these things for the record? In these documents we say:
>   WE WERE HERE, WE EXISTED, WE HAVE A DIFFERENT STORY

- Elæ [Lynne DeSilva-Johnson], Founder/Creative Director

RECENT & FORTHCOMING
OS PRINT::DOCUMENTS and PROJECTS, 2019-21

2021

Vidhu Aggarwal - Daughter Isotope
Steven Alvarez - Manhatitlán [Glossarium]
Johnny Damm - Failure Biographies
Power ON - Ginger Ko
Hypermobilities - Ellen Samuels [In Corpore Sano]
HOAX - Joey De Jesus [Kind*]
Ernst Toller's "Vormorgen" & Emmy Hennings - Radical Archival Translations -
Mathilda Cullen [Kind* / Glossarium; German-English]
Black and Blue Partition ('Mistry) - Monchoachi (tr. Patricia Hartland)
[Glossarium; French & Antillean Creole/English]

2020

Institution is a Verb: A Panoply Performance Lab Compilation
Goodbye Wolf-Nik DeDominic
Spite - Danielle Pafunda
Acid Western - Robert Balun

KIN(D)* TEXTS AND PROJECTS

Intergalactic Travels: Poems from a Fugutive Alien - Alan Pelaez Lopez
RoseSunWater - Angel Dominguez

GLOSSARIUM: UNSILENCED TEXTS AND TRANSLATIONS

Between Language and Justice: Selected Writings from Antena Aire
(Jen Hofer & John Pluecker))
Híkurí (Peyote) - José Vicente Anaya (tr. Joshua Pollock)

DOC U MENT

/däkyəmənt/

First meant "instruction" or "evidence," whether written or not.

noun - a piece of written, printed, or electronic matter that provides information or evidence or that serves as an official record *verb* - record (something) in written, photographic, or other form *synonyms* - paper - deed - record - writing - act - instrument

[*Middle English, precept, from Old French, from Latin documentum, example, proof, from docre, to teach; see dek- in Indo-European roots.*]

Who is responsible for the manufacture of value?

Based on what supercilious ontology have we landed in a space where we vie against other creative people in vain pursuit of the fleeting credibilities of the scarcity economy, rather than freely collaborating and sharing openly with each other in ecstatic celebration of MAKING?

While we understand and acknowledge the economic pressures and fear-mongering that threatens to dominate and crush the creative impulse, we also believe that *now more than ever we have the tools to redistribute agency via cooperative means,* fueled by the fires of the Open Source Movement.

Looking out across the invisible vistas of that rhizomatic parallel country we can begin to see our community beyond constraints, in the place where intention meets resilient, proactive, collaborative organization.

Here is a document born of that belief, sown purely of imagination and will. When we document we assert. We print to make real, to reify our being there. When we do so with mindful intention to address our process, to open our work to others, to create beauty in words in space, to respect and acknowledge the strength of the page we now hold physical, a thing in our hand, we remind ourselves that, like Dorothy: *we had the power all along, my dears.*

THE PRINT! DOCUMENT SERIES

is a project of
the trouble with bartleby
in collaboration with
the operating system